chi

CW01084397

Contents

A Parent's Guide to Handling Teenage Behaviour

taking your parenting to the next level...

INTRODUCTION

In recent years, an increasing number of parents from a wide variety of backgrounds have been asking for practical day-to-day effective methods of handling and controlling their teenagers' difficult behaviour. A lot of parents feel that they are always shouting at their teenager and although they are aware that it appears to have no effect, they are unable to find alternative methods of disciplining. Many parents fear that the shouting will escalate and they will end up hitting their child.

Feeling that their teenager is beyond their control contributes to parents' feelings of failure, guilt and despair. It is common for parents to become so bewildered by their teenager's behaviour that their self-esteem and confidence is further shattered by having to ask for help from outside the family. In seeking help, parents usually state that they have tried everything but nothing has worked. By this time the teenager has usually gained considerable power and may well be the controlling figure within the home. If there are two or more children causing this degree of disruption within the home, life can feel like an up hill struggle.

Many methods of discipline attempted by parents are in themselves very good but need to be used correctly and consistently in order to be effective. Few parents are aware that their teenager's behaviour may become worse before the chosen method of parenting becomes effective and therefore as a consequence, they abandon one method and attempt another approach. Social services departments, probation officers and youth offending team workers have become very familiar with these types of difficulties and for many years have sought to help and advise parents.

In order to help parents effectively manager their teenager's behaviour we have written this booklet. It is specifically designed for parents and is based on tried and tested practices.

Many thanks to the workers from Derbyshire Youth Offending Team and NCH Step-In Family Centre in Derby for their contributions, comments and evaluation during the development of the material. Particular recognition and thanks should go to the parents from Derbyshire (Julie, Wendy, Geraldine, Bridget, Michelle, Jayne, Pam and Jackie) whose hard work and commitment was invaluable.

WHAT WERE YOU LIKE AS A TEENAGER?

At times it is hard for parents to understand why their teenagers behave in the way they do. Parents shake their heads and sigh either feeling angry, bemused or both. We would encourage you at this point to think about what you were like as a teenager? What did you get up to? What did you wear? What were your friends like? What was your gang like? Where did you go? How did your parents deal with your behaviour? How did their actions make you feel?

Is your teenager's behaviour worse than yours was or is it that people and society reacts differently to it today than when you were a teenager?

Whilst remembering your teenage years you may begin to realise how normal your teenager's behaviour really is and it will help you to feel less anxious about it. You may even find yourself laughing!

JOB DESCRIPTION OF A PARENT

Think about what makes a good parent? What are the tasks involved? How different is it being the parent of a teenager to being a parent of a two year old? Many parents would say that there is little difference apart from the fact that you cannot put a fourteen year old under your arm and take them to bed, as much as you would like to sometimes! Here is a list written by a group of parents that describes the qualities and skills needed to parent a teenager.

A good parent must:
- Have a constant supply of money.
- Be quick in the toilet and bathroom.
- Supply food for them and their friends.
- Be able to stand the smell of cooking at 3 o'clock in the morning.
- Appreciate their clothes, music and sense of humour.
- Have no personal needs, e.g. privacy, TV programmes, outings etc.
- Be handy with hair straighteners, a mop and bucket (after nights out), stain remover and
- a needle.
- Be inconspicuous and when required must not acknowledgement them publicly.
- Be strong and firm at all times.
- Need little sleep and able to stay awake waiting for them to come home.
- Be fit enough to run around after them.
- Be a doctor, nurse and guidance counsellor whenever necessary.
- Be a shoulder to cry on, a good listener, a referee, and also have no opinions.
- Be able to shout.
- Be a telephone receptionist.
- Be a good organiser to meet everyone's needs.
- Like their friends and their boyfriends/girlfriends.

THE IMPACT THE MEDIA CAN HAVE ON FAMILY LIFE

Think about the images in the media and on the television that affect your teenager. Consider what pressures are out there. Observe the inappropriate images, read some of your teenager's magazines, listen to some of their music, watch some of their TV programmes. You do not have to like these things you just need to know about them.

When our children are small we control their interaction with the outside world. This is neither desirable nor possible when they are teenagers. As a parent save your energies for the things you can and should control. If you get the opportunity, ask your teenager what they think are the things that influence them. Discover what they are interested in. Do not be critical; just listen to them.

POINTS TO PONDER

Parents of teenagers have many questions which, if left unanswered, can leave them totally confused and very unsure of their ability to care for their children and young people. Some questions include: Is my child normal? What should I expect from my teenager? Should I feel the way I do about my teenager? What went wrong? The following statements are designed to alleviate some of your fears and anxieties.

a.   Being a parent is one of the most difficult jobs in the world but nobody teaches you how to do it.

Even those experienced in handling other people's children, e.g. teachers, nursery nurses etc. can have a sense of panic when they try to deal with their own children. Handling other people's children is no guarantee that they will be competent at handling their own. Time is given to teaching parents how to bath a baby, change a nappy but no one ever prepares parents for what comes next. For most parents it is a question of trial and error.

Some parents are fortunate enough to have a network of friends who they can turn to for help and advice, but for the majority of parents they only have people in similar situations to their own. This can lead to confusion and uncertainty. When people become parents they do not set out thinking that their child will become a difficult teenager, do drugs, offend, truant etc. It is not what parents plan so they are not prepared for it. Most parents have times when they struggle to cope with what their child presents. That does not make them a bad parent; it makes them normal.

b.   There is no such thing as a perfect parent. All parents make mistakes so do not compare yourself or your teenager to other families.

Most parents are hounded by an image of what a perfect parent should be or at least try to be. The majority of people believe the perfect parent should be: patient, trendy, a friend, strong and firm, not bothered about loud music and messy rooms etc. Do you achieve all of these things? Of course not, as there is no such thing as the perfect parent. All parents make many mistakes when handling their teenager's behaviour.

You may make a conscious decision not to parent your teenagers as you were parented, or you may decide that you want to follow the example of someone you admire, but the image of how you will approach things is often very quickly shattered. Many parents find themselves saying and doing things they promised never to do or say, e.g. "You will do what you're told because I said so" or "While I pay the rent you will do as I ask".

It is very common for teenagers to infuriate their parents, leaving them feeling disrespected and angry. Teenage behaviour can drive parents to become distracted and difficult situations can then follow in rapid succession, which results in parents losing confidence in their ability, feeling alarmed at their reactions, and depressed at the prospect of further years of struggle and failure.

If a parent has had a difficult time with their child when they were smaller, when the child reaches teenage years, the parent already has a bad image of themselves. It is important for parents to understand that most parents feel like this. If someone has a bad image of themselves as a parent, their self-esteem will be destroyed further by any mistakes they make when handling their teenager's behaviour. With a growing sense of failure, parents can begin to believe that there is something wrong with them as parents. It is important to remember not to lose hope!

On the whole young people are very resilient and can bounce back from situations very quickly. This very fact can be a great source of irritation to parents. Parents can blow their top and within a short space of time their teenager has forgotten about it while the parent is still fuming or feeling guilty.

The other mistake that parent's frequently make is that they compare their teenager to other teenagers. Any parent who has gone through the teenage years with their child will tell you that their friend's children have always been more polite to them than their own. This is a common experience.

c.   All children present problems throughout their lives.

The reality is that there is no such thing as the perfect teenager. They all misbehave, make mistakes, or present problems of varying degrees. The thing to remember is that they will probably continue to do so, even after they have left home. It can be very disheartening for parents to deal with one problem only to be presented with a new one soon afterwards. The periods of "problem-free" behaviour never appear to last very long. This is normal and is an indication that our young adults are testing out their surroundings and maturing. By the time your child gets to their teenagers years you can be exhausted, worn out and feel that you do not want to deal with any more problems. It is however vital that you keep going; your teenager needs your support, discipline, guidance and love just as much when they are 14 as they did when they were 4.

Think back to the "What were you like as a teenager?" section and about how your parents responded to your behaviour. Did it work? If it did, why did it? If not, why? What was helpful?

Think about what you want your teenager to be like. We have supplied The Perfect Teenager activity page as an example of the sorts of things parents say they wish for in their teenager. Look at it carefully and ask yourself if this is the kind of teenager that would be happy or normal, and then compare this teenager with your own. You really need to ask yourself, is there such a thing as a perfect teenager? If so, would you really want one? Teenagers are supposed to be challenging, play loud music and prefer their friends to their family; it is an important stage in their development.

Turn to page 7 and complete the empty cartoon image yourself. However remember to not be too unrealistic about your hopes. Maybe your teenager is doing a lot of good things that are overshadowed by the bad.

THE PERFECT TEENAGER!

Has a sensible haircut.

Is always pleasant and smiling.

Is always polite; never shouts or answers back.

Always hangs their clothes up and keeps their bedroom tidy.

Always leaves the bathroom clean after using it.

Does not keep asking for money.

Takes off dirty shoes before coming into the house.

Is always sensitive to other people's feelings.

Keeps their clothes clean.

Has a good level of cleanliness.

Uses tissues when necessary.

Never leaves dirty dishes in their bedroom.

Brings you cups of tea.

Remembers your birthday without prompting.

Is happy to cook a meal for themselves or for you.

Washes dishes without being asked.

THE PERFECT TEENAGER!

Use this activity page to write down all the qualities you think a perfect teenager should have.

d.   Most problems teenagers present are normal, but they do not need to be accepted.

When teenagers present problems it confirms that they are normal. This can be reassuring to hear as most parents think that their teenager's current behaviour indicates a problematic future. A parent's choice of punishment and its severity may be linked more to their fear of the future than the reality of the incident. It is important therefore that as a parent you think carefully about the way you deal with each situation. This thought links into the next section of the booklet, which helps you to identify different behaviour and the most appropriate responses.

YOU DRIVE ME CRAZY!

Make a list of all the things that your teenager does that you find annoying, challenging and difficult to handle. Below is a list of behaviours that other parents have supplied. See how this list compares to yours.

Teenagers drive their parents crazy when they:

- Refuse to communicate with them, but yet they are the life and soul of the group when they are with their friends.
- Have untidy bedrooms.
- Leave plates and unfinished food in their room for days.
- Leave washing on their bedroom floor instead of putting it in the linen basket.
- Change their image, e.g. wear lots of make-up, get tattoos or piercings, wear strange clothes etc.
- Come out with trendy phrases, e.g. "whack", "rude" or "major" and refuse to explain what they mean.
- Come home and go straight upstairs without even saying "hello".
- Slam doors if they have been told they cannot do something.
- Forget things.
- Lose their keys.
- Arrive home late.
- Miss their bus.
- Grunt instead of talk.
- Expect their parents to be mind readers.
- Stay out late.
- Are ignorant.
- Stay in bed all day.
- Think they know it all.
- Refuse to talk about things.
- Take clothes from their brother or sister's room but never admit to it.
- Make bodily noises.
- Are always on the phone.
- Expect you to feed all their friends.
- Ask for advice but any advice given is always wrong.
- Never put petrol in the car and leave it on empty for the next time you drive it!

All of the above are typical things that teenagers do and this list is very rarely different from one parent to another; be assured how normal your teenager is.

TYPES OF BEHAVIOUR

When parents are finding it difficult to manage their teenager's behaviour, it is common for them to get angry and treat their teenager with discontent. Look back at the list of difficult behaviour and you will see that some of the things on the list are less worrying than others, which consequently requires less discipline and effort on your part to manage.

It is useful for you to gain an understanding of the different types of behaviour and to recognise that the majority of things that teenagers do are not done deliberately to annoy their parents. The following are three areas of behaviour that all teenagers present at some time or another. The key to managing your teenager's behaviour correctly lies in determining which type of behaviour they are presenting, which consequently helps you to know how to respond correctly. The following three areas of behaviour are based on principles introduced by James Dobson in Dare to Discipline, Kingsway Publications, 1972.

1.   Teenage Irresponsibilities.

All teenagers do silly things that can make their parents angry or cross. It is common that they forget what they have been told because they are so preoccupied with other things, e.g. music, relationships, friendships etc. and sometimes they do things without even realising it. Some examples could include:

- They go out and they are enjoying themselves so much they forget the time and miss the bus.
- They lose the car keys.
- They leave things at home, in the pub, at school etc.
- They let their friends borrow their clothes and then forget who borrowed them.
- They borrow clothes and forget to give them back.
- They do not think about the consequences of their actions for others, e.g. they put the empty milk container back in the fridge and then they are amazed the next day when there is no milk for breakfast!

A parent's natural reaction to these incidences is "What did you do that for?" The teenager's response can be "What? I didn't mean to" or "Chill out! Get a life!" which then provokes anger from both side.

If a parent reacts badly to their teenager's irresponsibilities, it can cause the behaviour to become worse, destroy their child's confidence, or have a lasting effect on their relationship with their child. A good tip for managing this type of behaviour is to imagine how you would respond if it was somebody else's child. Often if the behaviour belonged to someone else's teenager you would not even consider shouting at them, you would probably laugh and say "Well that's teenagers!"

Generally teenagers do not do these silly things on purpose or to aggravate their parents; these things are nevertheless still very annoying. This type of behaviour needs to be handled, but it also needs to be looked at in relation to more serious aspects of behaviour. In other words you do not need to get cross, scream or shout; the best response is to guide, nurture and help your child to see the consequences their actions have on themselves and others. Try to keep calm and explain things logically.

Many parents feel relieved when they receive this information. It is reassuring that their teenager's irresponsible behaviour is not done on purpose. This can have an immediate effect upon their attitude and their method of handling this type of behaviour.

2.   Behaviour Linked to Teenage Development.

Parents can become very angry and frustrated with their teenager when they feel they should be able to accomplish a particular task. You must give careful consideration to your teenager's stage of development to ensure that they are able to achieve what you are asking of them. It is helpful for you to understand the typical stages of adolescence and the impact that puberty can have. A parent who understands this will be able to give better consideration to any problems that arise and can decide whether the teenager has actually developed the skills necessary to accomplish the task being set.

We all know that living with a teenager can have its ups and downs. The trouble is, even though we know that teenagers need to go through this difficult period in order to mature into adulthood, actually going through it is another matter! Teenage years are a stage in a child's development when they wonder, experiment and try out many aspects of life. Teenagers always want to reach their goal without going through the necessary experiences to get there.

The most difficult thing about living with teenagers is that in some aspects of their development they may appear to be very mature, for example sometimes teenagers can look a lot older than they actually are. Underneath this facade they may still be learning and functioning at a level that is lower than their age group, and still building their confidence in socialising and conversation. Examples of difficult behaviour may include:

- Mood swings.
- Being argumentative.
- Issues around hygiene.
- Changes in self-image, e.g. ear piercing, tattoos, clothes, etc.
- Hormonal changes & puberty.
- Loss of vocabulary that results in grunting.
- Changing from behaving like a 3 year old to behaving like a 33 year old.

All of these issues are linked to a teenager's stage of development and it is important to remember that none of these things are done deliberately to annoy us. This is the time when developmentally teenagers are trying to figure out who they are and what they want to be. They can also be vulnerable to negative influences from outsiders, which can affect the image of themselves and their self-esteem.

Teenagers are often unable to fulfil what we require of them without going through these developmental stages and learning through trial and error. Understanding the way that teenagers develop can be very intricate, in fact we all develop at different rates, and have different life experiences that will influence the way we mature, our understandings, and our view of the world, others and ourselves. The following may help you to understand your teenager's behaviour and put them in a more favourable light.

As young children grow up we know that there are six main areas of development. This does not stop when you become a teenager or indeed an adult; we are learning and developing all the time. The six main areas of development are known as:

S P I C E S

Social **P**hysical **I**ntellectual **C**ultural **E**motional **S**piritual
or
Self-Esteem

Social Development –

This is mainly how we interact with others and our skills in communication. Social development can often take a backward step during teenage years due to the changes that occur in some of the other development categories. Spending time with friends will influence what a teenage wears, how they walk and talk, the music they listen to etc.

Physical Development –

We are all aware of the vast physical changes that occur during the teenage years, some are visible and others are not. This category can often be the hardest for some teenagers and it can really affect their view of themselves. Body changes are difficult to adjust to and hormonal changes can create moodiness and anxiety.

Intellectual Development -

During a time when there are so many other developmental changes going on for a teenager, they are also going through the most vital part of their education. This can create enormous stress for some teenagers. Intellectual development also includes the growth of a teenager's life skills both educational and practical.

Cultural Development –

This category is not just about heritage and religion, it also includes the awareness of the values and beliefs surrounding daily life and how they impact on teenagers as individuals. The values and beliefs of other significant people in the teenager's life, e.g. friends, family, teachers, doctors etc. will also have an impact on their beliefs. It can sometimes feel they have forgotten what is important in life, e.g. they forget their manners, family life seems unimportant etc. This will change, hold on in there!

Emotional Development – This category covers areas such as caring, coping and empathy. Our emotional responses to different situations, e.g. bereavement, divorce, successes and failures, and the way in which we learn to feel and cope with them are the foundations for our emotional development. Emotions can be very acute and intense whilst going through the teenage stages, which parents sometimes find it difficult to understand.

Spiritual Development – or Self Esteem   This might appear to be related to religion but is primarily linked to the teenager's view of themselves and the world they live in. 'Who am I?' 'What do I want to be?' or 'What is it all about?' are common thoughts. This category links to the teenager's self-esteem, their views of themselves and the way others see them. It is vital to build a child's self-esteem in order for them to grow to their full potential, be happy and be successful.

Remember all teenagers develop at different rates. Do not compare your child to anyone else's as it only leads to unnecessary anxiety.

Another way of looking at this stage in your teenager's life is by relating it to a loss, e.g. the feeling people experience when somebody close to them dies and they are grieving. The following behaviours and feelings are common in somebody who is grieving:

- Their ability to perform socially, physically and intellectually is affected.
- They often feel lethargic, cannot be bothered to do much and want to sleep a lot.
- They feel emotionally insecure and do not have much confidence in themselves.
- They find it difficult to make decisions and to concentrate on anything.
- They begin to question their values and beliefs.
- They reflect on their relationships with others and their image of themselves.
- They do not want to be around people who do not understand; they seek out people who are going through a similar situation.

All of these feelings are also common feelings of most teenagers during this stage of their life. The best way to help them through this stage is to make them feel as secure as possible and help them build their confidence so that they can work their way through their social, physical, intellectual and cultural development at their own pace. It will be much more productive to guide and nurture your teenager through these types of behaviours rather than disciplining them. Eventually this approach will reveal the adult you are hoping for.

3.   Challenge to Parents' Authority.

This is the more difficult aspect of teenage behaviour. This type of behaviour is where the teenager is aware of their behaviour and the impact it is having but continues regardless. Defiance and stubbornness come into this category. Most parents have experienced giving their child an instruction that they expect to be carried out and the teenager takes a stand and says "No!" It may be that the parent has instructed them not to do something and they deliberately do what they have been asked not to. The challenge is "What are you as my parent going to do about it?" This is indeed the most serious type of behaviour and needs to be addressed and dealt with correctly.

Most parents back away from this type of challenging behaviour and consequently find that their teenager continues to challenge them more and more frequently. Parents need to take on this challenge and they need to win. If you accept that your teenager just refuses to do something you have asked, they will end up controlling you and treating you with contempt. The truth of the matter is that this sense of power can actually leave them feeling insecure, afraid of the power they have acquired and they will live their lives feeling out of control.

Parents who find themselves in this position need to develop skills that allow them to take back the control. When the parent does begin to take back the control, the teenager will still continue to challenge and test them, but they need to do this to see what their parent is made of and whether they really mean what they say. It is part of exploring and testing out life.

It is common for parents to overreact to some types of behaviour. Often they get confused between what is challenging behaviour and what are just stages of development or teenage irresponsibilities, e.g. when a parent screams and shouts about their teenager's untidy bedroom and demands they tidy up, most teenagers will dig their heels in and before they know it the parent has created challenging behaviour when in fact the untidy bedroom was actually linked to the teenager's stage of development, but by overreacting the parent has caused more challenging behaviour.

Most parents will discipline for 'teenage irresponsibilities' and 'behaviour linked to stages of development' but avoid dealing with the challenging behaviour because they do not know how to handle it. If you do not meet the challenges your teenager presents, you will just increase the number of challenges made. Teenagers need their parents to be safe, consistent and fair.

Most of the behaviours parents complain about usually fall into the first and the second categories (teenage irresponsibilities or behaviour linked to stages of development) and we should never discipline teenagers for these types of behaviours.

HOW DO PARENTS ENCOURAGE BEHAVIOUR THEY DO NOT WANT?

Before you look at how you manage the challenging behaviour, you need to think about other things that you can do to limit your teenager's difficult behaviour. Patterns of behaviour are habits, like crossing your legs or folding your arms. All habits are taught and teenagers learn their behaviour from many sources. They learn from peers, friends, media, but also from their parents. They listen, watch, imitate and test out, but they mainly learn from the reaction of others, including their parents, to what they do. In any behaviour there has to be a "pay off" for the teenager to repeat it. In other words it has to be worthwhile.

Think about who influences your teenager's behaviour? It may be certain friends, media, celebrities etc. Most of these things are out of your control but what you do have some control over is the influence you bring on your child. In other words the impact your behaviour has on them, what they are learning from you, the "pay off" they get from you etc. A parent's response can determine whether or not a particular behaviour continues. Remember all parents make mistakes and we all trip up in these situations. A typical list of things that parents might do that encourages difficult behaviour includes:

- Empty threats, e.g. *"You'll never go there again!"*
  "I'll kill you if you do it again!"
  "Don't think you'll be going out again 'coz you won't!"
  "Don't think you're too big for me to smack you".
  "You think you know it all but you don't".

- Letting things go for an easy life, e.g. *"I don't know why I bother!"*
  "There's no point telling you off, you never listen anyway!"

- Poor role modelling, e.g. shouting, swearing, smacking, drinking, smoking, violence, withdrawal of love, lack of interest etc.

- Sarcasm, ridicule and humiliation, e.g. *"No one will want you smelling like that".*

- Deferring to someone else, e.g. *"Wait till your mum gets home!"*
  "Your teacher won't be impressed with you when I tell him about this".

- Several punishments for the same thing, e.g. shouting at them, taking away a privilege, telling dad who then grounds them. This is unfair and it will just make your teenager angry; it will not stop their bad behaviour.

- Disciplining for 'teenage irresponsibilities' and 'behaviour linked to their stage of development'. The teenager will feel a sense of unfairness and subsequently will react in a challenging way.

- Not dealing with the challenging behaviour at all; doing nothing when you really need to be saying "No".

- Punishments which are too harsh, e.g. grounding them for six months, or doing things that might frighten or harm them.

- Respond differently when outside pressures affect us. This might include neighbours, family, media, e.g. *"We never did it that way when you were young".*
  "I heard a girl was attacked nearby, so don't think I'm letting you go out".
  "It's OK to let them play on the building site; they all do it round here".
  "Don't you think you're a bit 'over the top'?"

MANAGING THE CHALLENGING BEHAVIOUR

RULES

When thinking about dealing with challenging behaviour the starting point is to think about rules. When encouraged to think about rules parents are usually amazed at how many rules they have and how many they would like to add to the existing ones. Rules will of course vary from household to household, and even when teenagers are out of control there will always be one rule that they obey without fail. This particular rule is often linked to safety, e.g. always put out your cigarette properly, do not smoke in the bedroom, or do not smoke in the house.

This is a hidden source of strength in a parent and illustrates how effective you can be in some areas. What rule does your teenager never break? How do you make that happen?

A typical list of rules may include:
- Put the toilet seat down.
- Flush the toilet.
- Lock the door when you come in.
- Do not spend hours on the phone.
- Do not swear.
- Do not take drugs.
- Do not smoke.
- Tidy your room.
- Do your chores.
- Do not slam doors.
- Do not answer back.
- Come in when you are told.
- Keep the music at an acceptable level.

If there are two parental figures in the home, there is a need for you to be in total agreement about the rules you set or your teenager will quickly recognise the weakness and play one parent off against the other. If you cannot agree on how to deal with a piece of behaviour or a rule then agree to just allow one of you to manage that bit of behaviour and jointly manage other issues. Teenagers need some boundaries within which to operate. This helps to keep them safe at a time in their lives when there are lots of uncertainties. However it is important to remember:

- They need clear boundaries within which they can comfortably move.
- The rules only need to be around the challenging behaviour not the other types of behaviour.
- If you are experiencing a difficult time with your teenager a good tip is to ensure that there are clear rules around safety issues. The message you will then be giving will clearly be "I care about you", rather than, "I want to control you".

- The older the child, the fewer the rules, but they still need to be clear and achievable.

During difficult periods you may be tempted to increase the number of rules. This is not recommended as it just leads to conflict, confrontation and can cause damage to the relationship. Even with clear boundaries, teenagers will constantly test them out to see if they can alter them in some way.

Many parents have to come to terms with the fact that the love their teenager has for them, no matter how strong, does not include total obedience and full co-operation. Parents want their teenagers to become assertive, clear thinking adults who can make their own decisions and there has to be a learning process for this. Children can not walk as soon as they are born, they learn and they make mistakes along the way. This is the case with other skills as well.

HOUSE RULES

Complete this sheet with your teenager if possible. It is good to discuss and negotiate. Teenagers tend to conform if they feel they have had some say in decisions made.

RULES	NUMBER OF TIMES BROKEN
1.	
2.	
3.	
4.	
5.	

PUNISHMENTS

Now we have looked at rules we need to know what to do next when the rule is challenged. What do you currently do when your teenager breaks a rule? Make a list of the punishments you use. Below is a list of the most common punishments used by parents:

- Shout at them.
- Send them to their room.
- Ground them.
- Stop their pocket money.
- Increase their chores.
- Make them tidy their room.
- Stop them watching television.
- Send them to bed early and stop them having late nights.
- Stop them from seeing their friends.
- Stop them from seeing their other parent.
- Stop them having sweets, cigarettes, magazines, special activities, e.g. football match or going to a disco.
- Make them visit relatives.
- Threaten them.
- Make them answer you.
- Be sarcastic towards them.
- Ridicule them.
- Show them up.
- Humiliate them.
- Hit, smack, punch, grab, push them etc.
- Give them a good hiding.
- Lock them in a room.

PUNISHMENTS VERSUS CONSEQUENCES

When we get out of control or are unsure of what to do next we will often revert to harsher punishments which can be unnecessary or unfair. It is important that you take control in a calm manner.

Consider what the word 'punishment' means? Some common responses might be: harsh, tough, controlling, out of control, frightening, hurtful etc. Punishments generally benefit the person giving them more than the person receiving them. You must find the most positive way to discipline your teenager that will enhance your relationship overall. Teenagers know when their parents are not being fair and are out of control.

Look at the previous list and put a line through the comments that might come under the category of 'punishment' as these things will not work! Your aim must be to be consistent and fair, gain control back in a way that is not harmful and that will build upon your relationship with the teenager.

Consider the word 'consequence'. Consequences give us the impression of an automatic, planned result to a specific action. You should only be left with consequences on the previous list after crossing out all of the punishments. Consequences must be worked out in advance, specifically for each type of bad behaviour. You and your teenager both need to be aware of the consequences so when a consequence is being given, much of the emotion and heat is taken out of the situation. It is important to remember that what works for one teenager may not work for another, and an effective consequence can become a punishment if it is used too severely or inappropriately.

A good example of this is grounding. Often parents start by giving a whole week as the consequence. If you were to see these threats through every time, we could end up with the teenager potentially grounded for many months or even years. There is no point in saying something you cannot achieve; it will just take away your credibility. It is a good idea to offer a choice of consequence to the teenager as it takes out some of the emotion and helps to maintain the relationship.

Remember to only use a consequence that you are sure you can achieve. They should be small and irritating and something you can repeat without them becoming a punishment.

When children are young parents should use a method known as 'calm down time' as a consequence for their bad behaviour, i.e. getting their child to sit quietly at their side. This is not very easy to achieve when children become teenagers, but we can do something just as effective. We can use 'cool down time'. Often when our teenagers make us angry we dish out unrealistic punishments, e.g. 'Right that's it, you're grounded for the whole of the summer holidays!' Who is actually being punished with this consequence? Yes the parent is! Sometimes it is much more effective to say, "I need to take some time to think about what has just happened and what consequence will be most effective. I'll get back to you when I've had time to calm down". This is 'cool down time'. For the teenager the wait can be very effective in itself.

COOL DOWN TIME

As previously mentioned, if your child misbehaves when they are small you can use a number of ways to handle their behaviour which include removing them from the scene, placing them on a chair or on the bottom step, but preferably just holding them at your side until both of you have calmed down and cooled off. This is not likely to work with teenagers. Sending them to their bedroom may work but most teenagers voluntarily choose to spend time in their room so this might actually become a reward!

'Cool down time' is great for parents to use with their teenagers. It is where you remove yourself from the situation, perhaps by walking out of the room or by going into the back garden to take a few deep breaths and give yourself time to think. Some parents find shutting themselves in the bathroom for five minutes with the radio on can work well; this prevents the teenager from following you and stops them from continuing to talk about it while the situation is still heated. Where you go is not important, but removing yourself from the room they are in is. This will give you the time you need and will indicate that you disapprove of their behaviour.

HOW DO I WORK OUT WHEN TO DO IT?

First you need to decide what behaviour you will not accept; this may be different for each family. Examples include:

- You will not accept your teenager shouting or swearing at you.
- You will not accept being "bullied" into saying yes to something you are not sure about.
- You will not accept being pushed or poked.

When you have decided, you need to sit down and talk to your teenager about their unacceptable behaviour, but remember this must be done at a time when you are not angry.

WHEN DO I USE IT?

Once you have decided on the behaviour you will not accept you need to decide if cool down time is appropriate. For example, if your teenager truants from school, then going out of the room is unlikely to change that behaviour. However, if you want to change things such as shouting, temper outbursts or answering back, then 'Cool Down Time' can work.

HOW DO I USE IT?

Firstly you need to say what is happening, remind them that what they are doing is not acceptable, if they continue with the behaviour explain that you need to leave the room to have some time to think about the situation and you will talk to them about it when you have both calmed down.

Example Scenario:
"John you are shouting, please stop!"
If John continues, explain: "John, I don't want to be shouted at. I am going upstairs now. We will talk later when we are both calmer".

Example Scenario:
"Louise you're trying to make me say yes and I need time to think about it first."
If Louise continues to push you for an answer, "Louise, you are pushing me for an answer. I have told you I need time to think. I am going upstairs for 15 minutes. I will give you an answer when I come back."

Example Scenario:
Your teenager is out with his/her friends and they ring up asking to stay over at their friend's house tonight, "I need time to think so I'll phone you back in 10 minutes."

HOW LONG DO I USE IT FOR?

Without being too unreasonable 'Cool Down Time' can be for as long as you need, but you need to fulfil your promise and get back to them, for example:
"Are you ready to talk now we've cooled off?"
"Now that you are no longer shouting I'm ready to listen".
"I've made a decision about _____".

WILL IT BE DIFFICULT?

Yes, especially at first. Teenagers will not enjoy this and it may even increase the unwanted behaviour to begin with. This is normal and shows the strategy is working. You must not give in. You need to keep using it to succeed. This 'cooling off' method acts as a safety valve and it can be used with rude or cross adults too!

WHAT ELSE CAN I DO?
It is vitally important that as well as pointing out the unacceptable behaviour, you also need to give plenty of praise and make positive comments when your teenager presents acceptable behaviour, e.g. if they do not shout/swear at you or keep nagging you for an answer. Appreciating them when they respond in the way you want them to will help your teenager to learn and understand how you would like them to behave. Punishment may temporarily remove the unacceptable behaviour but it does not encourage them to adopt the behaviour we want.

THE THREE STEPS TO COOL DOWN TIME
STEP 1   Decide what unacceptable behaviour is. Discuss the behaviour and the consequences with your teenager. If the unacceptable behaviour occurs remember that it is your responsibility to correct it. If the teenager responds well you should praise them immediately.

STEP 2   If your teenager does not respond or responds badly, tell them you are going out of room until you have both cooled down and you will come back to talk about it soon. After the cool down period, you need to initiate communication again.

STEP 3   If the unacceptable behaviour continues, you need to go out of the room again until teenager is able to respond well.

POCKET MONEY

Another good consequence to use with your teenager is withdrawal of pocket money. When using this however it is important to remember the following:

• Decide on a total amount you would be willing to give them, e.g. £10.
• Agree on an amount that your teenager will receive regardless of their behaviour, e.g. £6. This means that if they behave themselves they could get an extra £4. Remember, never take away the whole amount as it will be viewed as a punishment by your teenager and could also make them resort to inappropriate ways of obtaining money, e.g. stealing.
• Inform your teenager that every time they break a rule you will deduct money from the remaining £4. The whole idea is to teach them what is not acceptable behaviour. Therefore, it is not sensible to deduct large amounts each time, e.g. if you deducted 50p every time they broke a rule they would only have 8 opportunities to learn that their behaviour was not acceptable. You should deduct small amounts; the more difficult your teenager's behaviour, the smaller the amounts you should deduct, providing more opportunities for your teenager to learn.

RULES, CONSEQUENCES AND CONSISTENCY

When trying to change your teenager's behaviour what you may find is that when you initially make a rule with a consequence it only seems to work for a short while, e.g. the rule could be working well between Monday and Thursday and then the weekend comes along and it all goes wrong. This is normal. Please remember that trying to change behaviour is a gradual and difficult process because there are so many things to think about.

1.   Once you have established the rules you want and need, you have to be sure that they are clear, age appropriate, not too severe, and understood by everyone.

   For example, you cannot say to your 16 year old,
   a.   "I want you in at a reasonable time!" What does that mean? It is not clear.
   b.   "I want you home from the disco at 9.00pm." This is not age appropriate and it is unfair.

2.   You also need to help your teenager keep to the rules by reminding and prompting them, e.g. "You're doing really well but do not forget what we agreed".

   You need to think carefully about the consequences. They must be outlined in advance and not suddenly come out of nowhere. We are all very good at losing our temper and saying, "Right then, that's it!" and doing something spontaneously. Consequences need to be small, boring and repetitive if they are going to work. You will not change behaviour if you use harsh and severe consequences. If you do make the consequences harsh and severe you will certainly do one, if not all of the following:

   - You will make your teenager angry as they are being unfairly treated.
   - You will make it harder for yourself to implement.
   - You are in danger of turning the consequence into a punishment.
   - You are in danger of damaging the relationship with your teenager, and a strong stable relationship is vital if your teenager is to feel safe during this difficult time in their life.

   Think back to the 'Pocket Money' section. If you take it all, or take large amounts away, you will create the scenarios above. A good thing to do with teenagers is to let them have a choice of consequence. If you do this you must remember that the consequences must be ones you can actually enforce and you will need to accept that they will chose the one which is most acceptable to them, e.g. give them a choice of which night they will be grounded. It is OK if they choose a night they were not planning to go out; you do not want to punish them, you just want to get them to think and therefore change.

3.   You need to be consistent; you need to present the same consequence in the same way every time the rule is broken. This is the most difficult bit and it is the thing parents are not good at for lots of reasons. Teenagers make you mad, tired, you get fed up, you cannot be bothered, you see it all as a waste of time etc. If you do not apply the consequence every time they break the rule your teenager knows that it is possible to get away with it

some, if not most of the time. They therefore play Russian roulette with you and will run the risk of getting a punishment because the consequence appears to come at random. Parents find it difficult to understand this and say things like, "My child takes no notice of me. I've tried everything and nothing works".

An example of this is the dirty cups and plates in the lounge. Parents generally moan about it to begin with, and then they pick them up themselves, or just leave them there and say nothing, or get angry and make them carry them into the kitchen. If you want your teenagers to put their plates in the kitchen you should make sure it happens every time and as soon as possible after the rule has been broken.

One of the mistakes parents make with consequences, is to increase them in the hope that they will work faster and make them into a "good" teenager quicker. Parents often look for the ultimate punishment for a quick fix. This is dangerous and unrealistic, e.g. a mother begins by saying to her 14 year old daughter that for every 10 minutes she is late she will have to come in 10 minutes earlier every night in the future. The daughter continues to come in when she wants to so the mother keeps reducing the time she can stay out. There is no initial effect so the mum decides not to allow her out at all and makes her stay in her room. The daughter climbs out of the window and stays out all night.

There are three major points that need to be highlighted here:

1. Parents believe that disciplining is the best method of changing difficult behaviour. This is not true. It is the hardest way and it is the most damaging in terms of relationships.

2. Once a consequence has been carried out you need to be mature and friendly with your teenager again. Do not carry it on, e.g. "I've not forgotten about yesterday".

3. A rule with a consequence which is consistently applied will change the behaviour you no longer want but it will not give you the behaviour you do want. Teenagers also need praise, acknowledgement and understanding.

CONSISTENCY IS IMPORTANT

It is vitally important that you consistently enforce your consequences because it helps your teenager:
- Learn that you mean what you say.
- To stop playing you off against another family member.
- Stay clear about your message.
- Learn you are always serious about this behaviour.
- Learn they are not going to get away with it!

Taking these points into consideration it is important to remember to:

- Consistently enforce the consequence every time the rule is broken.
- Ask your family, friends and your child's school to back you up.
- Try to plan how you will respond.
- Try to give appropriate responses, i.e. not something you cannot carry out, or something dreadful for a minor misbehaviour, or something too severe or inappropriate for their age.
- Try to always give the same response to the same misbehaviour.
- Try to make sure the teenager knows how you will respond if he/she misbehaves.

HOW DO WE GET THE BEHAVIOUR WE DO WANT?

We all want to like somebody, and we all want to be liked. This statement is very true. Think about who you like and why you like them and think about who your teenager likes and why. Remember it is normal at this stage in your child's life that they say they prefer other people's parents to their own.

Helping your teenager to feel positive about him or herself is very important and can have a positive effect on their behaviour. The scenario below gives a great example of this.

Example Scenario:
A teacher was very worried about her new class of ten year olds who had been labelled as the worst class in the school. She desperately wanted to improve their behaviour but she also wanted to do a good job. She started on the first day of term by saying to the class "Every time I see any of you doing something good, I am going to put a marble in this large sweet jar. On the day the jar is full we will have 10 minutes extra play time". Within one week the jar was full. She had put a marble in for very small things, e.g. smiling, sitting still for two minutes, little acts of kindness, putting their hand up when they wanted to say something, not shouting etc. The same children who were previously in the playground boasting about how many times they had been told off were now asking each other how many marbles they had got for the jar. They enjoyed being liked and praised for the good things they had done and as a result their behaviour continued to improve. The teacher is still operating this system, it is just a little more difficult to get a marble so they have to gradually try harder.

Going back to the pocket money scenario, there is a more positive way in which you could use it, e.g. rather than deducting money you could use it to add money. For example, you could say "You will definitely get £6 but for every time you are good I'll put you another 20p in your jar". As before you can have a limit of £10 but this way you are encouraging their good behaviour rather than punishing their bad behaviour.

What we know is that most people, especially teenagers, like attention and they will try to get it any way they can, either for their good or bad behaviour. What we also know is that if we see the good in people, it brings out the best in them and us! If you are struggling to relate to the nice things about your teenager try to concentrate on their good points for a while.

LIST ALL THE GOOD THINGS

Each and every time your teenager displays good behaviour write it down, it does not matter how small the act. This exercise will help you to remember all the good things about your teenager.

MONDAY

TUESDAY

WEDNESDAY

THURSDAY

FRIDAY

SATURDAY

SUNDAY

BRINGING OUT THE BEST

It is important that as a parent of a teenager you think about what kind of young person you want to raise. What kind of adult are you looking for them to become? Make a list of the qualities, traits, skills you would like your teenager to display. Once you have done this, then make another list of things that you can do to encourage this behaviour, e.g. praise, body language, respect, time together, financial rewards, etc.

Think about how you feel when someone praises you or smiles, and how much more effective that can be than a grand gesture. Good role modelling is essential when trying to promote acceptable behaviour in our teenagers. Do not make the mistake of bribing your teenager with rewards when you want behaviour to be repeated. Most parents get into bribing which is ineffective. The following provide a few practical examples to highlight the differences between inappropriate and appropriate rewards.

A bribe is something like this:
"If you tidy your room this week I will buy you a pair of trainers". This bribe is for the parent's benefit and although the teenager has a choice, they could even begin to bargain with you, e.g. they may respond with, "make it trainers and £5 and I might".

A random reward:
"You have been brilliant lately by keeping your room tidy so I've bought you those trainers you wanted". Random rewards can also be non-financial; sometimes a simple "thank you" works wonders. It is important for them to acknowledge that they cannot expect trainers every time.

An incentive:
"What would help you to do this because I know you want to do it? Is there anything I can do to help in anyway?"

The difference between a bribe and an incentive is that the former is for the benefit of the parent. The latter is for the benefit of the child. The message is that rewards need to be used properly if they are to improve behaviour. Used properly they can bring about massive changes.

Example Scenario:
A teenage boy of 14 years old was having major problems at school. He was disruptive and would not work, and despite his talent at sport he did not play. He was on report and all his teachers were very negative about him. His parents knew he was a good child; he was kind, caring and did not get into a lot of trouble but at school he seemed to be exactly the opposite. The parents had a meeting with the school accompanied by a friend who worked in the field of behaviour management. The worker was overwhelmed by the negative things surrounding this child. She asked all the teachers who had this child on report to write only good things on his report card for two weeks and to see how things went. Things were slightly better so they continued. After four weeks the teachers reported that his behaviour had improved and they were starting to like him. He was certainly starting to like himself. He joined the football team and began to try at his work.

We all like to be liked and if we are appreciated for the good things we do instead of being constantly punished or shouted at for the bad things, perhaps our behaviour will improve. One thing is for sure, our relationships with people around us will improve.

BEHAVIOUR TANK

Take time to look at the "Behaviour Tank" below. If you imagine that our behaviour is held in a tank in our body, half of it is our bad behaviour and the other half is our good behaviour. None of us are all good or all bad. Each side has an outlet pipe, i.e. if we give more attention to bad behaviour the good will pour out of the tank and vice versa. It is however important to recognise that it is not always easy to focus on good behaviour because when the young person is making us cross, our natural reaction is to focus on the bad behaviour.

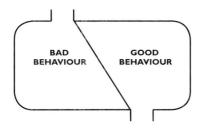

If you give too much attention to bad behaviour, you will end up with more bad behaviour.

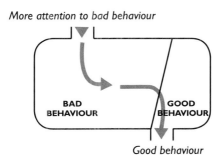

Reversely, if you praise your teenager for the good things they are doing, their bad behaviour will reduce.

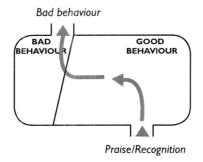

HOW TO AVOID DIFFICULTIES

1. The best way to manage difficult behaviour is not to let it happen in the first place.

    Parents are often the main instigators of bad behaviour especially when they are fed up with it or are expecting it, e.g. Mum is on her way home from work and her teenager has been at home all day. Mum is thinking, "What am I going to find when I get in? It will be the same as yesterday; empty coke cans, dirty plates. He'll be lounging on the sofa and the kitchen will be a mess. He'll have had his friends round all day". By the time she gets to the door she is ready to explode. She walks in and the scene is exactly as she imagined it. She immediately starts shouting and demanding that he tidies up. He just carries on watching TV until he cannot listen to her any longer, at which point he shouts back, gets up and walks out.

    Let's rethink this situation. Mum still knows what she will find when she gets home but tries to take a different approach. She comes in and perches on the sofa asking him what sort of a day he has had. She is positive with him at every opportunity. She says she feels like drink and asks if he would like one as well. He says yes so she says "Well ok I'll go and put the kettle on, why don't you bring those cups through to the kitchen and we'll make a drink together". With no confrontation and no shouting everyone feels better.

2. Showing an interest.

    Another way to avoid difficulties arising is to avoid boredom in your teenagers. Find out what they are interested in and try to ensure they have more time to spend enjoying these things. Alternatively you can find out from others how they can develop their interest, e.g. skating, swimming, guitar etc. There might be a local club or leisure centre nearby running courses.

3. The final thing to think about is stress management, not only for adults but also for teenagers.

    Living with teenagers is stressful for all adults. We need to recognise this and find ways of getting our stress levels down. Think of ways to do this, e.g. relaxation tapes, finding time to relax, breathing deeply, cool down time etc. It is also important to acknowledge how difficult it is for teenagers to change their behaviour. One good thought to hang on to is the fact that teenage years will not last forever!

THE TECHNIQUES YOU NEED WHEN DEALING WITH CHALLENGING BEHAVIOUR

The behaviour umbrella illustration below demonstrates quite simply the need to include all of the elements we have discussed. If one segment of the umbrella is missing then you will end up getting wet. Similarly if one of the segments of behaviour is not given attention, then the behaviour management will not be effective.

The message we want to highlight here for parents who are struggling with difficult teenage behaviour is, if they concentrate on rules and consequences they will increase conflict and encourage more difficulties. What you need to do is just have a few rules but give a lot of attention to the other segments, e.g. demonstrating correct behaviour, avoiding and preventing bad behaviour, giving praise and reinforcing good behaviour etc.

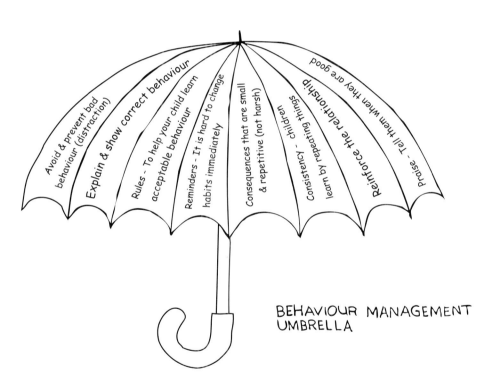

BEHAVIOUR MANAGEMENT UMBRELLA

THINGS TO LOOK OUT FOR

When you are dealing with difficult teenage behaviour there are certain things which you need to avoid and look out for which will help you to cope better.

a. Patterns of Behaviour. Most if not all good or bad behaviour has a pattern; it has a beginning, middle and an end. By identifying this pattern you are often over half way there in dealing with the behaviour. Sometimes it helps parents to identify a pattern if they write down or record the behaviour their teenager presents; three weeks is a good length of time to record.

Recording will require hard work especially if there are a number of children within the home. You need to know that there is not an easy route and need to be willing to tackle this. If you are prepared to do this you will need a lot of reassurance, praise and positive reinforcement from people around you. Take every opportunity to gain encouragement. Recording frequently produces some unexpected and interesting results. When reviewing the results, some parents often feel that the problem they thought was there actually is not. Recording enables you to see the behaviour in black and white without emotions overruling the situation.

You may find that your response to bad behaviour is either aggravating your teenager or maintaining the behaviour. This will give you an opportunity to adjust the way you handle the behaviour in order to get the desired outcome. For some parents, the behaviour is put in perspective and the real issues are highlighted.

Here are some notes on what to look out for when recording and some sample recording sheets.
- What behaviour patterns are emerging and how frequently?
- Which appears to be the most severe?
- Is the time of day or day of the week significant?
- Are the problems recorded childish irresponsibilities, behaviour linked to development, or a challenge to your authority?
- Does the child succeed in getting his/her own way?
- What punishment do you use?
- Are you consistent in handling the behaviour?
- Which method of punishment proved successful at some point during the recording?
- Do you show signs of getting angry before taking action?
- Are there any indications of positive reinforcement for good behaviour?
- Are there any other significant patterns of behaviour or handling emerging?
- Are there any specific periods of time or locations where behaviour problems are not evident?

>. One of the biggest problems parents experience is getting too emotional over their children's behaviour. Parents often agonise over situations, whilst their teenager has already forgotten about it or just does not seem to care less. Sometimes parents get so overwrought that they lose sight of the important issues and react totally inappropriately, yet if it was someone else's child they would handle it differently.

Example Scenario:
An 18 year old girl who had never truanted before decided to for the first time on the day of parents' evening. She went in to town with her friends to get breakfast and strolled into school at 11:00am. She had not missed lessons as she had two free periods. At open evening her mother was confronted by the head teacher about this incident. The mother was angry, confused and embarrassed and in front of the teachers she shouted at her daughter. The daughter stormed off feeling her mother was overreacting. What might she have done if it had been a friend's child or a child she did not know?

The message here is if you feel you are getting overwrought and stressed, stand back and take time out. Think, "What advice would I give if this was someone else's child?"

. Do not take on all of your child's problems.

Teenagers need to own their problems. Obviously they need help and guidance with big issues such as drugs, alcohol or offending, but smaller things like "I've got no money for the disco" you might want to respond "Have you thought how you can resolve this?"

RECORDING SHEET

DATE	TIME	WHAT WAS HAPPENING?	WHAT DID HE/SHE DO?	WHAT DID YOU DO?	ANY COMMENTS?

IMPORTANT POINTS TO REMEMBER

* Avoid confrontation as it makes everyone involved feel bad and unhappy.
* Do not be put on the spot; if you are not sure how to deal with it give yourself some time, e.g. "I'm not sure what to do about this, I'll get back to you".
* Privacy is important for all young people as well as adults. Try to get as much as possible for all of you.

THOUGHTS FOR PARENTS WITH TEENAGERS

Teenagers brighten up the home - they never turn the lights off!

Things you wish your teenager would say:
> "I want you to impart your wisdom and experience to me".
> "I don't think black is a good colour on me".
> "Is my music too loud?"
> "Let me pay my phone bill".
> "That's far too late! I'll be home a lot earlier".

When your teenager comes of age, employ a surgeon to be on standby to remove him/her from your wallet!

An education is what parents receive when they sit in on a conversation between teenagers!

The cleverest part of doing homework is thinking up the excuse!

It rarely occurs to teenagers that the day will come when they will know as little as their parents!

Why do teenagers not tell you where they are going? Because they don't know!

Adolescence is the time when your kids stop asking where they came from and start refusing to tell you where they're going!

Teenagers live in a world of their own - it is called boredom!

The trouble with life's questions is that when you're old enough to know the answers, you've forgotten the questions!

There is nothing like arguing with teenagers to realise that you're not young enough to know everything!

Teenagers are hormones with hair!

A teenager's natural habitat is in your pocket!

THE WHITE GARDENIA

Every year on my birthday, from the time I turned 12, one white gardenia was delivered anonymously to me at my house. There was never a card or note, and calls to the florist were in vain because the purchase was always made in cash.

After a while, I stopped trying to discover the identity of the sender, I just delighted in the beauty and heady perfume of that one magical, perfect white flower nestled in folds of soft pink tissue paper.

But I never stopped imagining who the sender might be. Some of my happiest moments were spent in day dreams about someone wonderful and exciting, but too shy or eccentric to make known his or her identity. In my teen years, it was fun to speculate that the sender might be a boy I had a crush on, or even someone I didn't know who had noticed me.

My mother often contributed to my speculations, she's asked me if there was someone for whom I had done a special kindness, who might be showing appreciation anonymously. She reminded me of the times when I'd been riding my bike and our neighbour drove up with her car full of groceries and children.

I always helped her unload the car and made sure the children didn't run into the road. Or maybe the mystery sender was the old man across the street. I often retrieved his mail during the winter, so he wouldn't have to venture down his icy steps.

My mother did her best to foster my imagination about the gardenia. She wanted her children to be creative. She also wanted us to feel cherished and loved, not just by her, but by the world at large.

When I was 17, a boy broke my heart. The night he called for the last time, I cried myself to sleep. When I awoke in the morning, there was a message scribbled on my mirror in red lipstick: "Heartily know, when half-gods go, the gods arrive." I thought about the quotation from Emerson for a long time, and I left it where my mother had written it until my heart healed. When I finally went for the glass cleaner, my mother knew that everything was all right again.

But there were some hurts that my mother couldn't heal. A month before my high school graduation, my father died suddenly of a heart attack. My feelings ranged from simple grief to abandonment, fear, distrust and overwhelming anger that my dad was missing some of the most important events in my life. I became completely uninterested in my upcoming graduation, the senior-class play and the prom-events that I had worked on and looked forward to. I even considered staying home to attend college instead of going away as I had planned because it felt safer.

My mother, in the midst of her own grief, wouldn't hear of me missing out on any of these things. The day before my father died, she and I had gone shopping for a prom dress and had found spectacular one - yards and yards of dotted Swiss in red, white and blue. But it was the wrong size, and when my father died the next day, I forgot all about the dress.

My mother didn't. The day before the prom, I found that dress waiting for me - in the right size. It was draped majestically over the living room sofa, presented to me artistically and lovingly. I may not have cared about having a new dress, but my mother did.

She cared how we children felt about ourselves. She imbued us with a sense of the magic in the world, and she gave us the ability to see beauty even in the face of adversity.

In truth, my mother wanted her children to see themselves like the gardenia – lovely, strong, perfect, with an aura of magic and perhaps a bit of mystery.

My mother died when I was 22, only 10 days after I was married. That was the year the gardenias stopped coming.

BY MARSHA ARONS